CAREERS IN

Computer Forensics

TERRY TEAGUE MEYER

ROSEN
PUBLISHING

NEW YORK

Published in 2014 by The Rosen Publishing Group, Inc.
29 East 21st Street, New York, NY 10010

Copyright © 2014 by The Rosen Publishing Group, Inc.

First Edition

Library of Congress Cataloging-in-Publication Data

Meyer, Terry Teague.
Careers in computer forensics/Terry Teague Meyer.—First edition.
     pages cm.—(Careers in computer technology)
Includes bibliographical references and index.
ISBN 978-1-4488-9593-9 (library binding)
1. Computer crimes—Investigation—Juvenile literature. 2. Computer science—Vocational guidance—Juvenile literature. 3. Forensic sciences—Vocational guidance—Juvenile literature. I. Title.
HV8079.C65M49 2014
363.25'968—dc23

                                                                    2012041358

Manufactured in the United States of America

CPSIA Compliance Information: Batch #S13YA: For further information, contact Rosen Publishing, New York, New York, at 1-800-237-9932.

Contents

Introduction   4

Chapter 1 What Is Computer Forensics?   6

Chapter 2 Computer Forensics and Local Law Enforcement   17

Chapter 3 Computer Forensics and the Federal Government   29

Chapter 4 Computer Forensics and Global Crime Fighting   40

Chapter 5 Computer Forensics Careers in the Private Sector   49

Chapter 6 Preparing for a Career in Computer Forensics   56

Glossary   68

For More Information   70

For Further Reading   73

Bibliography   75

Index   78

Since the popular television series *C.S.I.* first aired in 2000, stories about the professionals who work in forensics labs have become an entertainment staple for Americans. Forensics, the application of scientific methods and techniques to the investigation of crime, covers a very wide range of activities and careers. Television programs about criminal investigators usually feature those who deal with physical evidence, such as prints from fingers, shoes, and tires; bullets and the paths they might have taken; and, of course, autopsies of crime victims.

Less prominent on the screen, but perhaps more important in real life, are those who uncover and analyze information from computers and other electronic devices. Professionals in computer forensics (also known as digital forensics) can obtain information from distant locations and from far back in the past. They can retrieve erased or hidden computer files, determine the current and past whereabouts of suspects, and provide evidence of most types of criminal activity.

Outside the world of criminal investigations, these experts may work for government entities in such areas as intelligence gathering, anti-terrorism, and tax evasion. In the private sector, businesses may use computer forensics experts to protect their trade secrets and customer lists, spy on competitors, or simply improve the defenses of their computer systems and databases. Lawyers on both sides of criminal cases rely on the expert testimony of forensics professionals. In addition, law firms require the services of computer forensics experts in non-criminal cases such as personal injury, medical malpractice, and even divorce.

As computers and other electronic devices have become more and more enmeshed in the daily lives of Americans, computer forensics will have wider and wider utility. In the past, all bank robbers had to physically enter a bank in order to steal. Today, cybercriminals can steal vast amounts of money with just a few keystrokes. Computers make it easier to carry out crimes like identity theft and child pornography, and such crimes are on the rise. The spread of social networking has led to cyberbullying and malicious online activities unimagined just a few decades ago.

However, the same advances in technology that have given rise to computer crimes also provide law enforcement with a wide range of new crime-fighting tools and methods. For example, the popularity of global positioning systems (GPS) in smartphones and other devices has made it easier to track individuals and trace their whereabouts at any given time in the past or present. Computers and other digital devices store communications such as e-mails and texts and provide documentary evidence of Web searches and purchases. Digital forensics experts enable law enforcement, other government agencies, and those in the private sector to access this valuable information.

It is impossible to predict exactly where a career in computer forensics may lead, but it will surely offer growth and opportunities in the future. Many career opportunities exist in this field—in law enforcement, government, and the private sector. Certain basic techniques are common to all of these professional areas, but each also has its own unique and specialized strategies, methods, and goals. Exploring the different jobs and specializations within the field will show what education, training, skills, and techniques they require.

CHAPTER 1

What Is Computer Forensics?

Computer forensics is the discovery, collection, and analysis of data found on or taken from computer storage devices. Usually, such investigations are carried out in order to gather information and evidence that can then be used in a court of law. Unlike the forensic investigator dealing with physical evidence like clothing and bullets, the computer forensics expert is looking for evidence that is more or less invisible.

Anyone who has ever lost a research paper because of computer problems or a failure to save it correctly knows how easily a computer can conceal one's own information. Imagine the challenge of discovering and collecting data from another person's computer. Often, this data has been intentionally hidden, is protected by passwords, or is scrambled by encryption (code). Since the evidence may ultimately be used in court, it is essential to uncover and analyze the data without altering it in any way.

SECURING AND SAFEGUARDING DIGITAL INFORMATION

Some examples of situations requiring the services of digital forensic experts include damage assessment following an accident; criminal cases in which a suspect has stored information on a computer; and cases of fraud and deception, industrial

Federal digital analysts work at centers around the country to monitor the security of government computers and networks. They ensure that vital systems continue to operate in the event of a natural disaster or act of cyberterrorism.

espionage, and unauthorized leaking of corporate data. But the value of digital forensics techniques is not limited to criminal investigations. The ability to retrieve data lost through mechanical failure or user error is invaluable. American government, businesses, and power plants—almost all aspects of modern society—depend on computers. Therefore it is essential to keep computers and networks running smoothly and securely in spite of threats from natural disasters, cyberterrorists, and other criminals who might attack them. Computer security—working to protect data from theft and destructive programs, such as worms and viruses—is another important career path in computer forensics.

As digital storage devices have become more common in daily life, the term "digital forensics" is used to include not only computers but also cell phones, GPS, flash drives, and other storage devices. (The terms "digital forensics" and "computer forensics" will be used here interchangeably.) Computers, personal digital assistants (PDAs), cell phones, smartphones, and iPads and other tablets have become more widely used in society. As a result, retrieving and analyzing digital evidence has become even more important in solving crimes and obtaining criminal convictions.

Credit cards and bank ATM cards leave a trail of information about someone's whereabouts and activities. Public entities such as municipal transit and toll authorities can trace the timing of someone's movements through his or her E-ZPass or MetroCard usage. As our society has become more dependent on computer technology, cybercrime and cyberterrorism have increased as well. Digital forensic experts are ideally qualified to combat such menaces. Their expertise and forensic techniques not only help solve crimes. They also help prevent them by identifying and locating weaknesses in computers and networks and figuring out ways to prevent criminals and hackers from exploiting them.

The basis of computer forensics begins with an understanding of the digital world. Obviously, these professionals must have extensive knowledge of how computers work and how they are networked and communicate with other computers. Digital forensics specialists must become familiar with the various types of computer hardware, software, peripherals (devices connected to a computer, such as disk drives and printers), and storage media (such as hard drives, CDs, and DVDs). They must know how data is stored and how networks

Public transportation and toll authorities can track the movements and whereabouts of customers through digitally stored information on E-ZPass and MetroCards. Such information helps law enforcement gather evidence needed to solve crimes and bring cases to trial.

and Internet service providers work. Such expertise enables them to recover deleted or damaged files and copy files for further analysis.

COMPUTER BASICS

Most Americans are computer literate and know how to use computers and other devices such as smartphones. All of these digital devices are becoming increasingly user-friendly. But an understanding of digital forensics techniques must begin with the basics of how computers and digital devices operate.

A computer or digital device consists of hardware, which you can see, touch, and hold, and software, which is a program (or combination of programs) designed to give instructions to operate the computer. There must also be a power source, such as a battery or electrical cord. The computer is often attached to other related devices ("peripherals"), such as disk drives, printers, and video cameras.

The term "digital" refers to a system that represents information with the binary digits 0 and 1. These two digits can be programmed as a series of electrical "on" or "off" signals that can then be stored in computer memory. The basic unit of computer memory is a bit. This is short for "binary number," where 0 represents "off" and 1 represents "on." The next step up in computer memory is a byte. A byte (usually 8 bits) is the amount of storage space needed to store one character, such as a letter or single-digit number. Consider then that computer forensics examiners are charged with making "bit-by-bit" copies of computer and other storage media. That sounds somewhat like asking for a copy of a huge painting that meticulously replicates each brush stroke. The programs used to operate today's computers and other digital devices require a huge amount of computer memory. How much computer storage media can hold is measured in quantities like kilobytes (thousands), megabytes (millions), gigabytes (billions), and terabytes (trillions).

System software consists of the programs that control or maintain the operations of a computer and its devices. The most important of these is the operating system. There are many types of operating systems, since they are generally written to run on a certain type of computer. For example, the Mac OS X system will only work on Apple computers. Microsoft Windows dominates the software field and is used in many personal computers. Other important operating systems are UNIX and Linux. Most mobile and other consumer electronics devices have embedded operating systems contained on a single microchip. The operating system makes the hardware run. But a wide range of other software is needed to perform a variety of functions. These include managing different types of files, backing up data, operating printers, and maintaining computer security, to name just a few.

Computers require storage capacity space for the programs and instructions that keep them running and make them useful. The typical computer user is more interested in the storage capacity required for computers and other devices to be able to store his or her text, audio, photo, and video files. Business and government computer users input the characters that make up documents and files. These files can contain a wide range of information, including e-books, online banking and other business transactions, personnel files, and programs for operating automated systems from

HOW DIGITAL EVIDENCE CAUGHT TWO KILLERS

The serial killer known as BTK (short for his gruesome methods: bind, torture, and kill) terrorized Wichita, Kansas, beginning in 1974 and continuing for more than thirty-one years. After a long period of apparent inactivity, the murders recommenced in 2004. A task force was reassembled to hunt for the killer.

BTK enjoyed being in the limelight and taunting law enforcement about his ability to outsmart them. He began communicating with law enforcement by leaving notes and evidence of his crimes in packages around the Wichita area. Finally, he felt confident enough to send the police a floppy disk (the common form of portable digital storage at the time). BTK was actually Dennis Rader, an apparently model Wichita citizen who had recently been elected president of his church's congregation. Rader used a floppy disk from the church to send police the latest installment of his criminal diary. It took very little time to analyze the disk. Analysis revealed that the file was created by someone named Dennis and the disk came from a computer owned by his church.

Digital evidence also proved crucial in leading to the capture of Philip Markoff, known as the "Craigslist Killer," in 2009. Over a short period of time, Markoff attacked several women he contacted (on prepaid and untraceable cell phones) for dates through the Internet site Craigslist. After he killed masseuse Julissa Brisman, police were able to get an e-mail address for the victim's last client through a friend of hers. They used subpoenas to get the Internet protocol (IP) address of the client's e-mail account and the identity of the person who had opened it. The ten-digit protocol on his e-mail address led to Markoff's arrest a week after he made his appointment with Brisman.

Serial murderer Dennis Rader confessed to his crimes after digital evidence led to his arrest. He is serving ten life terms for murders carried out over decades.

power plants to manufacturing equipment. Private computer users require storage space for their music, video, photo, and Word files. Because there is such a wide variety of data to store and a huge range of needs among computer users, storage devices come in many different shapes and sizes. They range from the hard drive on a computer to the tiny magnetic strip on a credit card or MetroCard.

GROWTH AND CHANGE

Computer forensics is a very dynamic field, requiring experts to constantly broaden their knowledge and develop new tools in order to keep up with ever-changing technology. Consider that the software giant Microsoft releases a new operating system every few years, and cell phone manufacturers update their products even more frequently. In recent years, digital storage devices have assumed many new forms, with the trend toward smaller and smaller devices holding more and more data.

The National Institute of Justice notes that the advent of cloud computing, which allows users to create, share, and store files on remote, off-site computers throughout the Internet, has presented a new challenge for forensics experts. Law enforcement experts can no longer expect to find all of the digital evidence they need in one physical location, on one suspect's computer hard drive. The use of cloud storage would help child pornographers, for example, hide their identities and whereabouts, as they store images away from where they live or work and their home and workplace computers and digital devices.

A child shows off her GPS watch, designed to help her parents keep track of her. Using similar technology, law enforcement can trace the location and activities of criminal suspects through GPS systems in cars, watches, phones, and other digital devices.

Given the growing importance of evidence obtained from digital devices, it is likely that digital forensics experts will become more common in all areas of law enforcement. In July 2012, the *New York Times* reported that law enforcement requests for information from cell phone providers had increased from 12 to 16 percent over the previous five years. Cell phone service providers had responded to 1.3 million such requests in the previous year. These requests came in the form of police emergencies, court orders, and subpoenas to provide information. The information requested included calling history, calling location, and voice and text messages.

Law enforcement agencies report that global positioning systems, which are becoming a common feature built into phones, are proving to be critical in emergency situations such as kidnappings, shootings, and attempted suicide. Unless there is a change in this trend because of a change in laws (out of concern for personal privacy), it is very likely that this form of digital surveillance will increase along with the number of GPS devices people buy and carry. The same *New York Times* article reported that cell phone carriers were adding employees such as data technicians and phone specialists to handle the increasing volume of law enforcement requests for information. Such positions might be a good way to get on-the-job digital forensics training.

Law enforcement agencies at all levels—local, state, and federal—have a great need for computer forensics experts. Forensics of all types is essential to discovering and processing evidence that will lead to the capturing and prosecuting of criminals. But how do local law enforcement agencies use digital forensics to solve "traditional" crimes like theft, murder, and assault? What training do first responders need to ensure that they do not destroy or contaminate potential digital evidence? Is an entry-level position in law enforcement likely to lead to a specialization in digital forensics?

First responders to a crime scene must be aware of the proper way to handle digital evidence in order to preserve it for future analysis. Computers may be secured as evidence and provide a wealth of information in the form of e-mails, images, and video and audio files. In addition, they can provide a history of Internet searches, prove or disprove the whereabouts of an individual at a certain time on a certain date, and provide a record of purchases and banking transactions.

Law enforcement personnel may become trained in digital forensic techniques after they have begun their careers. Such training may take the form of professional workshops or boot camps. It appears likely that more and more first responders will be trained in this subject in the future, given the growing importance of digital forensics in crime fighting.

COLLECTING AND PRESERVING EVIDENCE

Local law enforcement personnel are likely to have the first contact with potential digital evidence relating to a crime. Depending on the situation, a first responder might have access to computers or phones at a crime scene. Alternatively, investigators might be authorized to seize such equipment based on a search warrant or subpoena. Whatever the situation, those who take possession of computer equipment or other digital devices must be extremely cautious so as to avoid damaging or altering digital evidence in any way.

FBI agents are shown taking away evidence to be analyzed and examined. First responders to a crime scene must be trained to handle computers and digital devices so that evidence is not contaminated.

In order to preserve digital evidence in the state in which it was seized, agents are trained to follow strict guidelines. Needless to say, law enforcement agents must keep computer equipment away from suspects and immediately determine if any software is running that might be intentionally destroying computer files. If data-destroying programs are detected, agents will turn off the computer. The next step is to photograph the computers and the entire scene and number the computers. Before moving any equipment, agents must shut the computers and other digital devices down properly, noting the time and date that each item was shut down and its location on the scene. The Regional Computer Forensics Labs of the Federal Bureau of Investigation (FBI) provide guidelines for handling seized material. This information includes photos to help novices recognize the different types of equipment and instructing them in how to shut them down properly.

Those first on the scene are cautioned not to turn on equipment that is switched off for fear of compromising evidence. They must even avoid looking at files on a computer that is found running. The FBI emphasizes that accessing computer files can uncover deleted files or activate encryption or destructive programs. It could also lead to charges of evidence tampering, which could make any evidence collected from the equipment useless and inadmissible in a court of law.

Instructions for handling different types of equipment vary. Windows, Apple, and other systems have their own unique characteristics, as do networked computers and laptops. Laptop batteries should be removed when collecting evidence and equipment. Removing the battery in PDAs or certain cell phones, however, will erase all of the data

Cell phones and smartphones provide all sorts of information about their owners. But special handling is required to preserve data to be used as evidence. Here someone at the Marshall University Forensic Science Center powers up a cell phone inside a radio frequency safe box.

contained within them. In some cases, more highly trained experts will be called in to handle unfamiliar equipment or networks. It is important to seize accessories such as power cords and cables along with other hardware. Carefully and properly packaging the equipment that has been retrieved is important in order to avoid damaging evidence through exposure to heat, magnets, radio transmitters, and the like. All of this must be done scrupulously and meticulously before beginning the actual forensic examination.

The rapid pace of change in digital technology translates into headaches for law enforcement and the need for ongoing training to keep up with new developments. For example, investigators have learned that they must put a smartphone or tablet on "airplane" mode immediately after seizing it in order to keep it from receiving new calls. If a confiscated phone did receive a call, it would affect the evidence because the device would no longer be in the same state as it was when it was seized. The validity of whatever evidence it contained could therefore be called into question. In addition, some phones, as a security measure, can be remotely accessed and all data erased. This feature is helpful for someone whose phone is lost or stolen, as personal information and sensitive data would not fall into the wrong hands. But for law enforcement agents, it's a problem because this security measure would allow a criminal to destroy evidence from afar. Some phones lose all information, such as the record of contacts and incoming and outgoing calls and texts, once the battery is removed.

The shrinking size of equipment and storage devices is another problem for law enforcement. USB flash drives (also called thumb drives, since one is about the size of an adult thumb) are able to store increasing amounts of data on a device that one can easily hide. As the storage capacities of thumb drives have increased to 2 to 3 terabytes of data, they can now store multiple servers and operating systems. Criminals can then remove the hard drive from their devices and operate everything from a thumb drive. When the computer, phone, or tablet is seized, investigators discover that there is nothing stored on them. Cloud storage is another means to hide digital evidence, as it enables users to store data away from the hardware that might be seized in a criminal investigation.

ANALYZING EVIDENCE

Mike Garrett is a senior police officer in the Houston Police Department and a member of the FBI Computer Crime Task Force. He works as a criminal investigator and is teamed with a forensic examiner. Garrett may be the first person to secure computers or other digital devices, but he will then turn them over to the digital forensics examiner. This person will copy the operating system and other files to be used as evidence. The forensic examiner will also provide technical information and expertise. For example the examiner might identify partitions on storage media and tell how much data they can hold. The examiner must do this without altering the original device, storage system, or files in any way.

The copy of the hard drive and its contents are then returned to the investigator who conducts a Case Agent Investigative Review (CAIR). While the investigator and forensic examiner may work together in the same office and work on the same evidence, they do not work collaboratively. Unlike television crime fighters who share opinions with their colleagues, real-life investigators are forbidden to do so. If investigators and examiners shared ideas, they might influence each other's opinions. It is important that each person examines the evidence objectively.

LOW-TECH FORENSICS TECHNIQUES

Much digital forensic examination requires special software or extensive computer science knowledge. According to Garrett,

PORTRAIT OF A COMPUTER FORENSICS INVESTIGATOR

Mike Garrett began working at the Houston Police Department as a young man in the mid-1980s, after completing two years in community college. His career began at about the same time as the Internet was born, so he had no way of knowing that he would end up working in the digital forensics

Houston senior police officer Mike Garrett also serves as a member of the regional FBI Computer Crimes Task Force. He often trains and assists law enforcement personnel in smaller municipalities over a multistate area.

field. He completed his bachelor of arts degree in criminal justice from Midwestern State University while working as a police officer.

Garrett has been working as a criminal investigator specializing in computer evidence for seven years, and he expects to continue in this position for the rest of his career. He moved into this position when an opening occurred. His previous work experience as an investigator made him a strong candidate. Over the years, Garrett had developed a valuable network of contacts in law enforcement agencies across the country while specializing in the investigation of confidence games ("con games") and swindles. Such criminals usually work in one area and then move on quickly to avoid capture and find a new batch of victims. By sharing information, law enforcement agencies can alert each other to con schemes and catch the criminals sooner. Work in computer forensics requires a similar amount of cooperation among law enforcement agencies, since digital information easily travels worldwide.

Garrett has acquired his computer expertise by attending continuing education courses while on the job. Continuing education is required of all Houston Police Department officers, but individuals have some choice in what they study. Garrett advises young people considering a career in this field to get a four-year college degree before seeking employment, as the degree leads to greater opportunities. A second piece of advice: Keep your record clean, and don't put anything on the Internet that you wouldn't want a future employer to see!

however, the best place to begin an examination is an obvious one: social media. Since computer forensics requires good deductive reasoning powers and the ability to think logically, try to think like an investigator for a few minutes about what a digital device could tell you about its user.

SOCIAL NETWORKING MEDIA

Social networking media includes sites like Facebook, Myspace, and dating sites. What is posted on these sites could provide photos of the individuals being investigated, their birth date, educational background, and list of friends. If the individual "liked" a cafe or gym, it might be possible to figure out where to find him or her. This kind of personal information would not even have to come from the individual's actual computer. Anyone with a Facebook account, for example, would be able to obtain at least some of this information.

Surprisingly, more than one criminal has boasted about misdeeds on a social media site and been turned in by friends and readers. Gang members are known to have their own Web pages and use social media to keep in touch with other members. In one case, a gang member posted pictures of himself holding weapons and claimed he was on a murder mission. He showed his tattoos and gave his gang name. By showing off online, he enabled investigators to easily identify and arrest him and seize a number of weapons and other gang material. Gang members have also posted videos on YouTube to boast of their exploits. Once the videos are in the public domain, investigators can access them and use them as evidence in court without first obtaining a search warrant.

Social media can also help bring about the arrest of gang members by making it easier to inform on them. An August 2012 article in the *Houston Chronicle* on the arrest of seven out of the ten most-wanted gang fugitives gave special credit to a new tipster Web site. The Web site had taken in 430 tips on gang activity within a 90-day period. People with information regarding criminal activity are often hesitant to report gang activity out of fear for their safety and that of their families. Because the Web site is anonymous, tipsters are protected from retaliation.

INTERNET SEARCHES

A user's history of Internet searches is stored on a computer unless it is purposely erased. Businesses use the Internet to customize ads based on users' past searches. Is it any wonder that law enforcement would do the same? A cookie is a sample piece of text from a Web site that someone has visited. The cookie provides a record or trail of where a user has gone on the Internet. Some cookies are stored temporarily, but others remain on the computer's hard drive until deliberately deleted. Records of users' search histories have shown where criminals bought weapons or other equipment used in crimes. Those planning crimes have also been caught researching things like how to make bombs, poison someone, or hire a killer.

E-MAILS

E-mail messages, of course, can provide direct evidence of what people are planning and thinking. Address books list contacts and associates. In addition, the full header (the address section) of an e-mail, which is not normally visible to those who send and receive e-mails, gives information about how the message was routed through Internet service providers (ISPs). Routing information can help locate the origin of a message. This can be very important, since criminals often hide their whereabouts and identities with fake addresses.

CELL PHONES

Cell phones also contain lists and phone numbers of associates for ready reference. Have you ever found someone's cell phone and figured out who it belonged to by scrolling through its contact list and dialing "Home" or "Mom" or "ICE" ("In Case of Emergency")? A list of contact numbers, recent incoming and outgoing calls, and text messages is readily available. With proper authorization, service providers can provide all sorts of additional information to law enforcement officials.

A smartphone or any device that contains a GPS can pinpoint the location of the person carrying it. An application on many devices that is designed to locate lost phones can also be used to find people. Gang members like to keep in touch, and many of them add a location to their tweets to share with their friends. However, rival gang members can take advantage of this to locate their enemies or set them up by intercepting tweets.

Of course, it would be difficult to analyze data that is protected by passwords or encrypted. Special software and expertise would then be needed to dig deeper into the secrets that a digital device might hold. Digital forensics examiners have a number of tools to assist them. Among the most widely known software packages are Forensic Toolkit, developed by the AccessData Company; BackTrack, for Linux operating systems; and EnCase Forensic. Such software is used not only by law enforcement but also in the private sector for computer security.

CHAPTER 3

Computer Forensics and the Federal Government

Computer forensics experts play a wide variety of roles in the service of the federal government. First, they represent federal law enforcement when assisting local, state, and regional police forces in solving crime and bringing criminals to justice.

Secondly, they help pursue those involved in cyber crimes—crimes carried out via a computer or over the Internet. Crimes like money laundering, distribution of child pornography, and theft of identities, money, and intellectual property have all become much easier to commit with the help of digital technology. Cyber crime in its many forms is often carried out by a network of criminals whose activities cross state lines and international borders. Therefore, investigating and prosecuting it requires the wide reach of federal authorities.

Maintaining computer security is a third essential function of federal computer experts, and the fourth is intelligence gathering.

COOPERATION AMONG LAW ENFORCEMENT ENTITIES

Movies and television shows often feature turf wars between local, state, and federal law enforcement, but in reality they cooperate in a number of ways. They share expertise, training, and even personnel. This cooperation has increased a great deal since the 9/11 terrorist attacks and following the 9/11 Commission Report of 2004. For example, there are now seventy-two fusion centers, one in every state, plus twenty-two in major urban areas.

Fusion centers act as information clearinghouses. They receive threat information from the federal government, analyze that information, and send it to local agencies. They also gather tips, leads, and reports of suspicious activity from these same local agencies and channel them to the appropriate federal agencies. Fusion centers help law enforcement agencies with security clearances, funding, and shared training, technology, and technical support. Needless to say, these centers require the services of computer forensics personnel.

Since the FBI can only handle federal crimes, its cooperation with local and state agencies can benefit everyone but the criminals. For example, a federal official may want to prosecute someone for drug trafficking but need more time to process evidence. He or she may fear that the suspect might flee the country in the interim. Local law enforcement might prevent this by arresting the suspect for drug possession or even traffic violations.

To make cooperation among agencies easier, Congress has approved the use of task forces that share training and may deputize local law enforcement agents to assist them. Mike Garrett of the Houston Police Department, for example, is a task force officer assigned to assist other agencies—not just the FBI, but also smaller police and sheriff departments in a multistate area. This is very useful in prosecuting child pornography cases, as the FBI must show evidence of a certain number of images (which might take a long time to uncover),

New York City police officers and FBI agents talk at the site of a search for evidence in the disappearance of a young boy. Cooperation between local and federal law enforcement is essential in fighting crime, including those crimes that have a cyber component to the evidence and its collection.

while local and state officials can review a smaller number of images on-site and make immediate arrests. On the other hand, since much cyber crime is international, local and state authorities need the help of federal agencies to extend their reach beyond the limits of their jurisdictions.

Federal agents work closely with local and state law enforcement to provide training and sophisticated facilities and expertise that would otherwise not be available to cities and counties. While local law enforcement may seize a suspect's digital equipment and participate in investigations throughout the arrest and courtroom phase of a crime, the forensic examiner has a different role. Certified examiners at the FBI's regional or national computer forensics labs not only copy data but also carry out a thorough independent examination of potential evidence. These experts can recover passwords and then use them to decode protected or encrypted files. Examiners can determine the type of data files on a device and compare these with known documents and files. They can recover deleted files, determine when the files were created, and convert them from one format to another. By analyzing files based on searches of keywords and phrases, they might be able to supply evidence of the planning of a robbery or murder-for-hire, for example.

From the standpoint of someone looking for a career in computer forensics, this overlap in law enforcement personnel can be both confusing and helpful. Where to find the best entry point would depend on where you are starting out in terms of education and geographical location. Such positions within the federal system would require at minimum a four-year college degree. However, one could qualify for a local or state position with only two years of college.

COMPUTER SECURITY

Digital forensics experts are also needed to protect and secure the vast network of computer systems that enable the federal government to operate. Although computer security is not exactly the same as computer forensics, both require much the same education, knowledge, expertise, and skill sets. And the use of this expertise in the area of digital security opens up many more career avenues to anyone interested in this field.

The federal government could not do without computers to gather data, issue funds for everything from Social Security checks to highway construction, and provide information to government entities, businesses, and individual citizens. Computerized systems help planes take off and land safely and guard our air space. All of these critical computer systems are vulnerable to attack.

Paul Brenner worked for years as inspector general of the nation's electronic intelligence service, the National Security Agency (NSA). In his book *America the Vulnerable*, he points out that computer systems have become vulnerable, in part, because people want to be more easily, quickly, and broadly connected to more information sources. Brenner states that the resulting pressure to increase computer connectivity "creates a dilemma because the more widely and quickly you make information available, the more trouble you have protecting it." He further notes that the cost of becoming an Internet thief is very low. Some hacking tools can be downloaded for free. Thieves who know how to steal information but don't know how to use it for their own profit can simply sell the information they obtain (like credit card or Social Security numbers) to existing criminal organizations who know how to (mis)use it.

Hacktivists (hackers who wish to draw attention to certain social or political issues), criminals, and foreign governments use the weaknesses of computer systems for their own purposes. According to a 2012 editorial in the *New York Times* written in support of legislation under debate in Congress, the director of the U.S. Cyber Command reported that intrusions against computers that run essential infrastructure increased by a factor of seventeen between 2009 and 2011. The editorial reported that American businesses lose billions of dollars annually through cyber attacks and that two hundred attacks (some successful) were attempted on power plants, electric grids, water treatment plants, and the like throughout 2011.

In order to protect computer data and systems, all areas of government and private industry must maintain a vigilant watch against the threat of cyber intrusions that could lead to theft of data or computer malfunction. According to the *CBS Evening News*, FBI veteran Shawn Henry estimates that cyber criminals and state-sponsored foreign hackers try to breach American computer systems millions of times each day and are often successful. Needless to say, computer security experts are needed to identify and shore up the vulnerabilities of federal government computer systems.

How do these intrusions take place? One method is "spearphishing." This tactic involves the sending of a fake e-mail message that appears to come from a trusted source. Someone receiving such an e-mail could allow an intruder to access an entire computer network just by clicking on a link or attachment contained within the misleading e-mail.

MALWARE

Malware, short for "malicious software," refers to any program that acts without a user's knowledge to deliberately alter the way a computer operates. Such programs come in many forms. They can harm a computer by making it run slower, fill up available memory, add new files and programs, remove existing ones, and cause operating systems to shut down suddenly or fail to start up. If you have been the victim of any sort of malware, you already know what annoyance and expense it

A computer forensics specialist with the Virginia State Police is examining a computer hard drive. Digital forensics expertise requires continuing education, as hardware, software, and malware are constantly evolving and advancing.

can cause. Imagine the damage it can cause in a large facility such as an oil refinery, transportation hub, highly sensitive military or nuclear installation, or communications center linked to a national or international computer network.

There are several types of malware. A computer virus infects a computer in much the same way that a cold or flu virus infects a human. The computer virus spreads throughout the computer system and may damage files and software, including the operating system. A Trojan horse, named after the ancient Greek story, hides within the computer and may appear to be a normal program until something triggers it to disrupt the host computer in some way. A worm is a program

FIGHTING CYBER CRIME

The FBI's "Ten Most Wanted" list is well known. But you may not know that the federal law enforcement agency maintains other lists of most-wanted fugitives, including one devoted exclusively to cyber criminals. In recent years, this list included seven fugitives, all of whom had lived or operated in the United States, and all but one with a foreign connection. Their crimes? One is an indicted child pornographer. Two worked together to hack into computers and create disruptions. They would then sell useless software to their victims in order to "fix" the problems that they had created. Between 2006 and 2008, they had been charged with defrauding consumers of $100 million, which was quickly transferred to overseas bank accounts. Others on the most-wanted cyber criminal list had been charged with money laundering, identity theft, bank fraud (opening fake accounts or hacking into credit lines in order to transfer money out), and setting up an auction site that took people's money but gave them nothing in return. This cyber-oriented most-wanted list offers a good overview of the types of crimes that computer forensics experts combat daily.

that copies itself endlessly, thereby using up memory or resources in a computer or network, eventually causing it to shut down. A rootkit hides in a computer and then allows someone from a remote location to take charge of it. Certain personal computers can be taken over and turned into "zombies" and then assembled into systems called botnets. These are home and business computers that are infiltrated, taken

This federal cyber security analyst works at the Malware Laboratory in Idaho. Such experts are on the alert for new types of malware. They also look for weaknesses that make computer systems and networks vulnerable to cyber attacks.

over, and made to operate like an army of cyber robots. The botnets are operated by automated programs that send out e-mail spam, pry into and steal financial information, or spread malware to even more computers.

As computer experts try to bolster security and close vulnerabilities, hackers, cyber criminals, and foreign spies are working just as fast to break through any new defenses that are erected. A wide variety of computer security and digital forensic software is available over the Internet. While this software was first developed for use by information technology systems administrators to protect their data, it is now also being bought by hackers and cyber criminals who study it in order to identify any chinks in the anti-malware armor.

HACKERS

The term "hacker" originally referred to someone who was skilled at writing computer programs or who programmed as a hobby. But for some time now, the term has referred to a person who breaks into computers or systems for malicious reasons. In the world of hackers, there are "black hat hackers" and "white hat hackers," so called because in old black-and-white western movies the bad guys wore black hats and the

This demonstrator at a protest in Berlin, Germany, is wearing a mask representing the hacker group Anonymous. Hacker attacks can now both originate from and spread to any location throughout the world.

good guys wore white hats. But the line between them is somewhat blurred. Some hackers known as "hacktivists" feel that they are doing nothing wrong. They believe that they are simply exposing the need for greater computer security and, in so doing, are performing a public service. Others are doing it for the thrill of a daunting challenge and out of a sense of mischief.

In his book that recounts his exploits, *Ghost in the Wires*, Kevin Mitnick describes himself as the "world's most wanted hacker" and expresses pride that he never tried to profit from his skill at breaking into telephone systems. While still a teenager, he got his start by "phreaking," meaning that he figured out how to make long-distance calls for free. He didn't connect stealing telephone service with theft. But the authorities did, and he was eventually caught and sent to prison.

Perhaps the best-known hacker group is Anonymous. One of its goals is to keep the Internet free of regulations. When the document-leaking Web site WikiLeaks published a large number of State Department cables, legislators called on businesses such as Visa, MasterCard, and PayPal to cut ties to the site. To punish these companies for complying with the government's demands, Anonymous launched a series of cyber attacks against them. Some suspected members of the group have been arrested for these and other, similar operations. But it will be very hard to put an end to such groups. The nature of the Internet helps keep them connected and anonymous.

CHAPTER 4

Computer Forensics and Global Crime Fighting

When it comes to computer security and cyber attacks, there is really no boundary between foreign and domestic crime-fighting operations, since computer systems and the Internet have truly created a global community. Much computer crime is facilitated by international networks. Similarly, the Internet has enabled terrorist groups, hate groups, child pornographers, and others to connect and communicate with like-minded criminals around the world. Consequently, many government-based computer forensics careers have international reach, even for individual professionals who never leave a desk or lab in the United States.

The basic tasks and strategies of computer forensics experts are much the same whether their focus is on domestic or foreign criminals and hackers. In this section, we will focus on two challenges shared by computer professionals at home and abroad and on the role of computer forensics experts in the intelligence-gathering community. Outside our borders, computer experts are needed to protect American embassies and military and other sensitive installations around the world. Computer experts are essential to intelligence-gathering activities within the military and agencies such as the Central Intelligence Agency (CIA) and the National Security Agency (NSA).

CRACKING THE CODE

Two ways to hide information on computers and digital devices are through encryption and steganography. Encryption is the

Experts man their stations at the Threat Operations Center inside the National Security Agency (NSA) in Fort Mead, Maryland. The NSA is among a number of federal agencies that need digital forensics experts.

act of turning information into a code so that it cannot be read or understood. A secret key or password to the code will "unlock" the hidden meaning. In order to keep sensitive data safe, computer software is used to encrypt the files. You may not be aware of it, but Web sites that have addresses beginning with "https" instead of "http" are so marked because they use an encryption method developed by Netscape called Secure Socket Layer (SSL). SSL protects the privacy of the Web site and the individual user. Software is also needed to unlock encrypted files. The more complicated the key, the more likely the code cannot be broken. In 2002, the U.S. government adopted an Advanced Encryption Standard using key sizes of 128 to 256

Encryption and code breaking are specialties of the NSA (www. nsa.gov). Its Web site has information about preparing for a career with the agency.

bits (assuming 8 bits equals one character, that would be 16 to 33 characters long).

Although computer professionals in many agencies are experts in dealing with encryption, cryptology (the study of codes) is the specialty of the NSA. The NSA sponsors a number of educational outreach programs to interest young people in this area of expertise. In 2011, it announced the launch of the NSA CryptoChallenge, a mobile game app available for free through the Apple App Store. The app is designed to educate young people about career opportunities within the NSA by challenging them to decode hundreds of puzzles that test pattern-recognition skills.

Steganography is a method of hiding computer-encoded data within a transmission of unrelated data. This is a bit like using a book with a hidden compartment to hide valuables. Steganography takes advantage of gaps or unused spaces in computer files, filling them with encrypted transmissions. Authorities would see an innocent-looking message, but the intended receiver would understand that the message contained encrypted material to be decoded. In an article in the online magazine *Dark Reading*, Kelly Jackson Higgins reported on the discovery that a hacking enterprise known as Operation Shady RAT (RAT stands for "Remote Access Trojan," a type of malware) used steganography to hide malicious code or data behind image files. Computers infected with this RAT were commanded to report back to their control-and-command server. But these commands were concealed as bits in images. What appeared to be a picture was actually a form of malware on the attack.

A form of steganography is actually used to protect against the crime of digital piracy. The same technique may be used to place a secret or disguised identifying characteristic, like a hidden trademark or serial number, in order to protect copyrighted materials such as software or music and video files. This use of stenography is often known as "fingerprinting" or "watermarking." It is a mark of authenticity, just like the watermarks on currency.

INTELLIGENCE GATHERING AND CYBER WARFARE

The purpose of intelligence gathering is to discover and reveal potential threats to national security in order to prepare for

PREPARING FOR YOUR BACKGROUND CHECK

Any law enforcement job will require some sort of background check. For jobs in the intelligence community and many other federal agencies, expect a long and very thorough background check. Local and state law enforcement will require you to have a clean criminal and financial record. Expect to pass a drug test as well.

What sorts of activities would prevent someone from pursuing a career in computer forensics? Laws vary from state to state. But felonies or crimes of "moral turpitude," such as prostitution and minor drug offenses, would likely be a problem. Charges such as driving under the influence (DUI) of drugs or alcohol might also bar an applicant from a position. DUI has long been considered a serious offense, but law enforcement is now also recognizing the danger of distracted driving. Traffic violations and fender benders are not surprising among young drivers. Now that law enforcement agencies are aware of the dangers of texting while driving, they will likely look into the records of potential recruits to make sure that their accidents were not caused by distracted driving.

Attention has focused in recent years on the popularity among teens and young adults of "sexting." Young people who sent photos they thought would be kept private have had their reputations and even lives ruined when others made the photos public. In some places, sexting is considered a serious crime: the production of child pornography. Anyone with any interest in working in a position that requires a background check must think before dashing off a message or image. Once someone hits "Send" or clicks "Post," the user loses control of the content that he or she has posted, forwarded, or sent. Given the flexibility of today's communication devices, a private text could become public in a moment. And once text or images are out there on the Internet, they remain public forever.

Another crime that young people may not consider all that serious, since it is so widely violated, is theft of intellectual property such as movies and music. Selling pirated material is a felony, and buying it is also illegal. Anyone thinking about becoming an agent should avoid buying, selling, and sharing pirated media.

them or render them harmless. Computer security threats are a relatively new phenomenon, but the threat of hostile attacks by enemies or terrorists has been with us for a long time. Intelligence gathering has traditionally been used to prevent physical attacks on national interests and American soil, such as those on Pearl Harbor in 1941 and the World Trade Center and Pentagon in 2001.

One immediately thinks of the CIA and NSA as the nation's primary intelligence-gathering agencies, but other federal agencies do this as well. A Web site for the American intelligence community (http://www.intelligence.gov) lists seventeen different agencies and offices that work independently and together. These agencies are not taking a passive role in maintaining national security. In a June 2012 article in the *New York Times*, David Sanger reported on how the United States, working with Israel, had launched cyber attacks on Iran's nuclear development program. The cyber weapon program, code-named "Olympic Games," was started under the administration of President George W. Bush and continued by President Barak Obama. It remained a closely guarded secret until a programming error caused the American and Israeli-designed malware to escape and spread throughout the Internet to computers around the world.

According to the *New York Times* article, the United States did not admit having developed cyber weapons until 2012. It still has not admitted to using them. However, Sanger explains in great detail how the Olympic Games project was carried out. A "beacon," or intelligence-gathering program, was introduced into Iran's Natanz plant to provide information on how the plant operated. Based on the beacon's information, a computer code fifty times as big as a typical computer worm was developed and eventually introduced at the plant through a thumb drive.

The worm, later known as "Stuxnet," hid in the system and launched a number of computer attacks, destroying a number of centrifuges designed to purify uranium. Because the attacks were so random, the Iranians could not figure out what was destroying their equipment. The report on this effort quotes Michael Hayden, a former CIA chief, as saying that this was the first use of computers to destroy equipment. Previous attacks would only slow down computer systems or steal information. But then Stuxnet escaped from Natanz because of a coding error. It migrated from a centrifuge to an engineer's computer. Once that computer was hooked up to the Internet, Stuxnet began replicating itself and spread around the world.

Iranian technicians monitor operations at a nuclear power plant. A computer worm, Stuxnet, penetrated the computer network of Iranian nuclear facilities and caused tremendous damage to equipment.

The Stuxnet story shows the power of cyber weapons and the dangers that they pose. Iran reported in 2012 that it had been attacked by another intelligence-gathering virus called "Flame." Iranian officials suspected that it, too, had been developed by the Israelis. Clearly, cyber weapons will continue to be important to national security, both as a threat and a counter-threat. During the Cold War period in the second half of the twentieth century, the United States and the Soviet bloc conducted a conventional and nuclear arms race. One can imagine a cyber arms race developing in the future, as countries strive to combat computer programs that are becoming more and more complex, powerful, and destructive.

Since programs such as these are meant to be secret, anyone working in this area would need top-secret security clearance. In fact, anyone hoping for a career in computer forensics should plan ahead and make sure that their criminal record—and their digital footprint—remains absolutely spotless.

CHAPTER 5

Computer Forensics Careers in the Private Sector

Many different types of businesses offer careers in digital forensics. The same computer expertise and techniques needed by law enforcement and government agencies are required in the private sector as well. Private-sector jobs may offer higher salaries and be easier to find, as federal careers are regulated by a highly structured system of civil service. What are some of the career options that private businesses offer?

PRIVATE INVESTIGATORS

Private investigation and security firms carry out many of the same functions as law enforcement. A private investigative firm can gather evidence, including digital evidence, just as police do. One might wonder why anyone would pay for an investigation that law enforcement would conduct for free. Oftentimes a police investigation moves too slowly or stalls because there is not enough evidence to move forward in a criminal case.

Consider this fictional situation, based on actual private investigation cases: Betty, the bookkeeper for a construction company we'll call "BuildCo," meets Roy, a subcontractor, through her position. Betty and Roy become romantically involved and figure out a scheme to pay for their honeymoon in Tahiti by stealing from Betty's employer. This is done by

A digital security expert working in the private sector discovered a worm attacking a social networking site. A link masquerading as a picture unleashed a virus that passed personal information about users back to the worm's creator.

overpaying Roy's company for work that he performs as a subcontractor. Suspicions arise when Betty leaves the company, and her successor notices that Roy's company has been paid much more than other subcontractors had been for similar work. When a private investigator is called in, he is able to uncover hidden computer files, including e-mails in which Betty and Roy discuss their plans to cheat Betty's employer. Their resulting prosecution might be aided by forensic auditors. These are accounting experts who analyze financial data to uncover evidence of criminal and suspicious activity.

The employer could have notified the police, but they might not have pursued the case very aggressively, since the criminal activity was only suspected and more urgent matters affecting the broader public may have taken precedence. Had the police caught the wrongdoers, they could have prosecuted them and had them thrown in jail, but BuildCo would not have been much better off. By calling in a private investigator and suing Betty and Roy in civil court, BuildCo would be in a better position to recover funds lost to the scheming pair.

Private investigators are also needed to gather evidence in non-criminal legal situations. In cases of family legal issues such as divorce, child custody, and arguments over who inherits Aunt Mary's fortune, computer forensic evidence could help establish timelines and uncover hidden assets. Such services could be invaluable to law firms as well as individuals. Law firms might also use forensics professionals to provide information needed to defend clients in criminal cases or bolster personal injury or medical malpractice cases.

SAFEGUARDING PRIVATE NETWORKS, SYSTEMS, AND DATA

Like the government, corporations large and small must take digital security seriously and pay for experts to keep their systems and data safe. Digital forensics can help recover essential data lost through natural disaster or system failure. Corporate systems and networks are also under attack from cyber thieves looking to steal everything from customer credit card numbers to employee Social Security numbers. Hackers and cyberterrorists unleash destructive malware either for political or personal reasons, as well as for profit. Consequently, companies must be alert to weaknesses in security. Digital forensics experts can help in boosting security measures and detecting problems such as employee theft or the leaking of trade secrets.

Software companies and Internet and telephone service providers need to be constantly on guard for security weaknesses in their products in order to protect their customers—and their reputations. Another problem for many kinds of businesses is piracy. Publishers, filmmakers, those in the music industry, and developers of software and games all expect to profit from their creative efforts. Meanwhile, media

These are examples of equipment used to make counterfeit DVDs. Piracy of intellectual property is a global problem requiring cooperation among law enforcement around the world.

and music pirates—and many ordinary consumers—assume that whatever they can download is theirs, free for the taking. Trying to keep ahead of hackers and cyber criminals is a constant battle, due to the rapid pace of technological advancement. For this reason, experts in computer forensics and digital security frequently meet to share ideas. This industry requires constant learning and updating of one's skills and knowledge, so an interest in continuing education is essential for anyone who wants to enter digital forensics.

PEN TESTING

Taking a proactive approach to digital security, those in both the public and private sector use penetration testing ("pen testing") to uncover weaknesses in computer systems and networks. A pen tester attacks the system just as a cyber criminal would in order to find evidence of system weakness or vulnerability that will be used to correct potential problems and prevent attacks from outsiders. All companies need to protect their systems and data. In addition, many companies that do business with the Department of Defense or carry out sensitive research in biotechnology risk losing big government contracts if their computer security is found to be lacking.

The SANS (SysAdmin, Audit, Network, Security) Institute trains and certifies information security personnel. It includes penetration tester on its list of "top gun jobs." The SANS Web site says of pen testers: "You can be a hacker, but do it legally and get paid a lot of money!" It describes this job as one suited to someone who enjoys puzzle solving and big challenges. In his book *The Art of Intrusion: The Real Stories Behind the Exploits of Hackers, Intruders, and Deceivers,* former hacker

PUTTING HACKING SKILLS TO BETTER USE

Government agencies and private entities alike combat hackers and cyber criminals by taking a proactive approach called penetration testing, or "pen testing" for short. Pen testing is, in effect, authorizing someone to try to hack into a system so that he or she can identify and reveal any weak spots. Pen testers need to think like the people who infiltrate and ransack computers and networks for criminal reasons in order to help develop better ways to keep intruders out. Pen testers are authorized to do what they do. Others who call themselves "white hat hackers" or "ethical hackers" do much the same thing for their personal amusement. They claim that in doing so they are performing a valuable service by calling attention to security weaknesses.

Kevin Mitnick devotes a whole chapter to pen testing and describes what it involves. Because pen testers often do things that might appear improper or illegal, they must get a written agreement from a client showing that they are authorized to perform their aggressive digital probing and attacks. Without the proper authorization, they would look a lot like "black hat hackers."

Pen testing may involve more than computers. It also often tests the human weaknesses present within a computer network. The computer network's users are often the weakest

Computer experts solve problems and troubleshoot at the SANS Institute. This organization provides specialized training. It also certifies the qualifications of those working in the fields of digital forensics and computer security.

link. A security breach is often the result of human error, such as using default passwords or allowing unauthorized personnel to enter buildings. Kevin Mitnick carried out many of his security breaches by using social engineering. Typically, posing as an insider, he would call up someone and trick him or her into giving him information that helped him gather still more information that should have been confidential. He and others also used fake company ID badges. The fake badges would not actually open doors. Instead, the hackers would wear them and walk into the back doors of buildings after lunch. Others, seeing the badge (and no doubt violating company security rules) would hold the door open for them.

CHAPTER 6

Preparing for a Career in Computer Forensics

Preparing for any career should start with an honest and clear-eyed examination of one's interests, talents, and personality traits. Aptitude tests and a talk with a school counselor are good places to start a quest for self-understanding and career planning. You probably have a keen interest in computers or you wouldn't be reading this book. A career in computer forensics will obviously require problem-solving skills, patience, and attention to detail. It will also require some sort of higher education, a bachelor's degree in computer science being the most likely path. If you are truly committed to a career in computer forensics, you can make it happen one way or another.

LAYING THE GROUNDWORK

While still in high school, or even middle school, young people can choose classes and participate in clubs to help prepare for a career in digital forensics. A good place to begin is in math class, as math is the foundation of computer science. Obviously, anyone interested in a career in computers should take computer science courses as early as possible. The availability of computer science and higher mathematics classes varies widely from school to school, as well as among districts and states. Depending on where you live and go to school, you may have limited opportunities to study computer science. If your school doesn't offer many computer-related

High school and community college math and computer science courses provide a good foundation for specializing in computer forensics.

courses and extracurricular clubs, consider taking courses at a nearby technical school or community college. Also check to see if your local public library or community center offers any computer skills and programming courses.

Math clubs, science clubs, and computer science interest groups are also great places to expand one's digital knowledge and experience outside the classroom. Participation in groups such as Odyssey of the Mind encourages young people to work together, use their individual and collective creativity, and develop problem-solving skills. Even those in schools with limited opportunities in this area can find a world of information online. Professional organizations such as the Association for Computer Machinery (ACM) and the American Society for Engineering Education (ASEE) have online programs and information for young people. The National Science and Technology Education Partnership even sponsors an online program of peer-to-peer math tutoring. Many of these organizations sponsor competitions and/or summer programs and provide scholarships to enable students to attend them. Getting involved in competitions and enrichment programs in middle school or high school can lead to recognition and, more important, scholarships to help pay for college.

GOVERNMENT CAREER-BUILDING RESOURCES

The U.S. Department of Labor sponsors several Web sites that are extremely helpful career-planning tools. They are useful for people changing jobs, veterans leaving military service, and young people just starting to think about the future. O*NET is the nation's primary source of occupational information. It includes a career and jobs database that is constantly updated. Through O*NET, users can find out the prospects for growth in a wide range of careers. One can browse careers by criteria such as level of preparation required (both in education and experience), field and job title, and the future demand predicted for such positions.

The O*NET site includes a vast array of resources for career planning. O*NET Academy offers webinars and audiovisual presentations explaining how to use its resources. Another section, "My Next Move," features an interactive tool that can help someone who is not sure exactly what he or she

FINDING A JOB OR INTERNSHIP WITH THE FEDERAL GOVERNMENT

The federal government is a tangled network of departments and agencies, each with a bewildering string of initials and acronyms that can be confusing for someone looking for a job, internship, or educational program. Looking at the organization chart for the Department of Justice (DOJ), one finds the FBI, the Drug Enforcement Administration (DEA), and the Bureau of Alcohol, Tobacco, Firearms, and Explosives (ATF). These are all likely landing spots for those interested in computer forensics. Also in the DOJ, the National Institute of Justice provides a wealth of digital forensics services and information.

Meanwhile, the Department of Homeland Security, which includes a number of important agencies, features cyber security careers and internships on its Web site. The Central Intelligence Agency (CIA) is a separate entity that is mainly concerned with intelligence gathering. The NSA/CSA (National Security Agency/Central Security Agency) is another independent agency whose focus is on code making and code breaking. The Web sites for these agencies focus on recruiting professionals in cyber security and cyber forensics. It offers a wealth of information regarding career offerings and internships. For example, the NSA offers a work-study program open to high school seniors in the Baltimore/Washington, D.C., metropolitan area. Every year, talented students get paid to work part-time as computer aides using the NSA's sophisticated data-processing equipment.

The federal government helps job seekers navigate this maze of employment information with a one-stop job information clearinghouse and application center: http://www.jobs.usa.gov. A recent search of this site for opportunities in computer forensics turned up two with the National Aeronautics and Space Administration (NASA), one with the Department of State, one with the Department of Commerce, one with the Federal Trade

Commission, one with the DEA, several positions for forensic accountants in various agencies, and three with the military. Clearly, a job seeker would miss out on many federal opportunities if he or she only looked into agencies such as the FBI and CIA.

It is also a good idea to search for jobs using a variety of keywords such as computer forensics, digital forensics, computer security, and others to bring in more results. The job information supplied on the federal government's central jobs Web site is very detailed, including information about salary and benefits and complete requirements for application. There are phone numbers and numerous links to resources that can help applicants. The Web site also features a Pathways program to help students and recent graduates find internships and obtain entry-level positions.

wants to do. This is an excellent resource for young people thinking about the future. By ranking one's preferences in sixty work-related activities, the tool creates a kind of interest profile and then matches the user with career possibilities based on those interests. By clicking on a given career, one finds details including salary, outlook for growth, and educational and experience requirements.

Other helpful Department of Labor resources are the *Occupational Outlook Handbook,* which includes much of the same information as O*NET, and CareerOneStop. The latter includes hints for job seekers and links to sites like state jobs banks.

EDUCATIONAL REQUIREMENTS

Like everything else in the digital world, the educational opportunities in computer forensics are constantly changing. Currently, there are around fifty higher-education programs in the United States and Canada. A few colleges and universities offer bachelor or master of science degrees in computer forensics. The majority, however, offer lower-level associate's degrees, concentrations, or certifications in digital forensics and/or computer security. There are also a large number of online courses offered by for-profit and vocational schools. The number of programs is likely to grow, and the prospective student should consult a high school counselor before enrolling.

A two-year program might be the quickest and cheapest way to get into a meaningful position and gain actual experience in the field (and perhaps acquire further academic education and training at the employer's expense.) However, a bachelor's or master's degree in areas such as computer science, engineering, math, technology management, and even accounting might be the most direct route to a career in computer forensics in either the public or private sector. A four-year degree is required for jobs with federal agencies, and many also require a master's degree. There are many organizations and private facilities that offer specialized training and certifications in digital forensics as well as other areas of computer expertise. Examples include SANS Institute and GIAC (Global Information Assurance Certification). Like local law enforcement, the FBI and CIA offer extensive training to those they hire.

Online resources provide detailed information about job openings and requirements for applicants. Broaden your search by looking at sites like O*NET, which has links to a large number of federal agencies, including the Drug Enforcement Administration (www.justice.gov/dea).

An entry-level law enforcement position can lead to a career in computer forensics. An associate's degree (two years) in criminal justice would prepare someone to be hired by local law enforcement. The *Occupational Outlook Handbook* indicates that law enforcement positions only require a high school degree or the equivalent. Many police departments have their own academies (about twelve to fourteen weeks in length) that provide the additional training and hands-on experience needed before starting the actual job. Once employed, you can focus on workshops and on-the-job training that would prepare you for a specialization in computer forensics. Sam Houston State University's Center of Excellence in Digital Forensics conducts forty-hour boot camps to train law enforcement agents in the basics.

TAKING THE MILITARY ROUTE

Military service can also lead to careers in computer forensics and is a good option for those who cannot easily afford college. The military will accept high school graduates as young as seventeen (with parental consent). ROTC (Reserve Officers' Training Corps) programs in many high schools and colleges offer students scholarships and a head start in the military upon graduation.

Like other federal government departments and agencies, the U.S. military is huge and complex. The four basic branches—Army, Navy, Air Force, and Marines—are just the start. The National Guard and Coast Guard offer other possibilities to serve. These various branches of the military have full-time and reserve options. All have need of computer security support. The Department of Defense, which oversees all of these branches (except the Coast Guard, which is part of the Department of Homeland Security), maintains a helpful Web site called Today's Military. The site links to each branch of the military and offers an overview for those who are considering joining the military. Topics include joining the military, boot camp, compensation (salary and benefits), and career fields. The Department of Defense also includes a Cyber Crime Center of its own, known as DC3.

In order to determine each person's personal strengths and abilities, the Department of Defense has developed a battery of eight individual tests, which together make up

Department of Defense forensics examiner Gil Moreno studies several hard drives associated with a crime. A career in the military is one of several ways to become a computer forensics expert.

the Armed Services Vocational Aptitude Battery (ASVAB). Students can take these tests as early as tenth grade and can take them more than once. The results of these tests guide where a recruit is directed for training or service. Of course, the individual has some choice in these matters, too.

Joining the military is not an easy way to get an education. It is a way of life that requires commitment, sacrifice, and dedication. The length of time commitment varies, but a new recruit should expect a minimum of eight years of service (although four years might be on reserve rather than active duty).

EXPERIENCE AND ONGOING TRAINING

An alternative to an educational concentration in computer forensics would be community college or vocational training in a more general area of computers. This could lead to employment as a computer service technician or technical support person. Both areas are projected to have faster-than-average growth, and such positions might offer on-the-job training and paid continuing education. A recent search of computer forensics and computer security job offerings on professional Web sites showed a number of positions that did not mention educational requirements, only skills and experience.

Someone who is really good with computers might wonder if becoming a hacker is a good way to prepare for a career in digital forensics. It would certainly be an extremely dangerous and ill-advised way to gain experience. Hacking is

This woman works for Protegga, a private computer forensics, e-discovery, and data collection service based in Dallas, Texas. Protegga utilizes state-of-the-art forensic tools, years of investigative and technological experience, and precise methodologies and procedures to identify, collect, analyze, preserve, and recover evidence. It employs only experienced, certified, and licensed computer forensics experts who know exactly how and where to find the evidence hidden in even the farthest recesses of a digital device.

illegal and, depending on what network is attacked and in what manner, it can be a federal crime that is punishable by a long sentence in federal prison and massive financial penalties. Former hacker Kevin Mitnick is now a best-selling author and computer consultant, and the equally notorious Kevin

Poulson gave up hacking for journalism. However, both of them also served time in prison for their crimes.

Would-be hackers have many new, positive, and socially productive outlets for their energy and creativity. In 2011, the National Cyber League was created. This group gives college teams a chance to test and expand their skills in cyber security. The Department of Defense's DC3 sponsors an annual Cyber Crime Challenge. Competitions like this are bound to increase in number as government agencies try to foster talent and encourage young people to enter this critical field. Maybe you'll be competing in years to come!

Glossary

bit The basic unit of computer memory, where 0 represents "off" and 1 represents "on."

byte The amount of computer storage space needed to store one character (usually 8 bits). How much computer storage media can hold is measured in quantities like kilobytes (thousands), megabytes (millions), gigabytes (billions), and terabytes (trillions).

cloud storage An off-site storage system maintained by a third party.

cookie Information stored on a user's computer at the request of software operated by a Web site that the user has visited. Web sites use cookies to recognize users who have visited them before.

embezzlement Crime in which an employee steals from an employer, usually by manipulating financial records and misappropriating company funds.

first responder A professional such as a police officer or firefighter who is the first to reach the scene of a crime, emergency, or natural disaster.

identity theft Any type of crime in which the criminal uses another person's personal information to commit acts of fraud or deception. Identity theft became a federal crime in 1998.

intellectual property An idea, invention, or process that derives from the work of the mind or intellect; an application, right, or registration relating to this.

intelligence gathering Seeking out and collecting often secret and sensitive information that has military, political, or commercial value.

Internet protocol (IP) address A unique string of four sets of numbers separated by periods that every computer or network is assigned on the Internet. It's a digital signature unique to each computer and network.

malware Any sort of malicious software used to enter a user's computer without permission in order to steal, disrupt, or destroy its files, operating system, or software. Examples of malware include worms and viruses.

money laundering Engaging in activities to hide money acquired through criminal means. For example, illegal funds might be transferred overseas or deposited into the account of a legitimate business.

operating system The system programs that allow a computer to operate and perform its elementary functions.

protocol The means by which a computer communicates with another computer; for example, hypertext transfer protocol (http).

software Programs that run on computers, including the operating systems that make them run.

subpoena A court order requiring a person to appear in court or present desired documents for court review. Such an order may be needed to enable law enforcement to seize digital devices.

universal resource locator (URL) The Internet address of a file. It has three parts: a protocol, a host, and a file name.

Universal Series Bus (USB) flash drive Also known as a thumb drive, this is a storage device about the size of an adult thumb. It is a handy way to transport data.

For More Information

American Society of Engineering Education (ASEE)
1818 N Street NW, Suite 600
Washington, DC 20036-2479
(202) 331-3500
Web site: http://www.asee.org
The ASEE focuses on education in engineering and math. It produces a number of publications for professionals, students, and teachers. It also cosponsors the Science and Engineering Apprenticeship Program.

Association for Computing Machinery (ACM)
1515 Broadway
New York, NY 10036
(800) 342-6626
Web site: http://www.acm.org
The ACM is a professional organization that supports people in the computer field and those preparing for such careers. It includes student members and sponsors student competitions.

Communication Security Establishment Canada (CSEC)
P.O. Box 9703
Ottawa, ON K1G 3Z4
Canada
(613) 991-7110 (IT Security Learning Centre)
Web site: http://www.cse-est.gc.ca

The CSEC is Canada's agency charged with protecting electronic information security. It provides technical assistance to law enforcement and security agencies.

Institute of Electrical and Electronics Engineers (IEEE)
2001 L Street NW, Suite 700
Washington, DC 20036-4910
(800) 678-4333
Web site: http://www.ieee.org
The IEEE provides publications, conferences, and education to advance careers in engineering and computer science. Its Web site includes information on pre-university career preparation.

Internal Association of Computer Investigative Specialists (IACIS)
P.O. Box 2411
Leesburg, VA 20177
(888) 884-2247
Web site: https://www.iacis.com
The IACIS is an international, volunteer, nonprofit corporation composed of law enforcement professionals dedicated to education in the field of forensic computer science. It focuses on training and certification.

Royal Canadian Mounted Police (RCMP)
73 Leikin Drive
Ottawa, ON K1A 0R2
Canada
(613) 993-7267

Web site: http://www.rcmp-grc.gc.ca
The Royal Canadian Mounted Police is Canada's national
    police service. Its Technological Crime Program, with
    headquarters in Ottawa and offices throughout the
    country, is staffed with computer forensics experts who
    support crime fighting throughout Canada.

U.S. Department of Labor
200 Constitution Avenue NW
Washington, DC 20210
(866) 487-2365
Web site: http://www.dol.gov
The Department of Labor gathers statistics about jobs and
    careers. It also sponsors a variety of Web sites and provides
    links to current information about careers, including
    salaries, academic and experience requirements, working
    environment, career advancement, and projected growth.

WEB SITES

Due to the changing nature of Internet links, Rosen Publishing
has developed an online list of Web sites related to the subject
of this book. This site is updated regularly. Please use this link
to access the list:

http://www.rosenlinks.com/CICT/Fore

Arata, Michael J., Jr. *Identity Theft for Dummies.* Hoboken, NJ: Wiley, 2011.

Bowden, Mark. *Worm: The First Digital World War.* New York, NY: Atlantic Monthly Press, 2011.

Brezina, Corona. *Careers in Law Enforcement.* New York, NY: Rosen Publishing, 2010.

Evans, Colin. *Criminal Justice: Evidence.* New York, NY: Chelsea House, 2010.

Farr, Michael. *Top 100 Computer and Technical Careers: Your Complete Guidebook to Major Jobs in Many Fields at All Training Levels.* 4th ed. Indianapolis, IN: JIST, 2009.

Farrell, Mary. *Computer Programming for Teens.* Boston, MA: Course Technology, 2008.

Ferguson. *What Can I Do Now?: Computers.* New York, NY: Infobase, 2007.

Furgang, Kathy. *Money-Making Opportunities for Teens Who Are Computer Savvy.* New York, NY: Rosen Publishing, 2014.

Gerdes, Louise, ed. *Cyber Crime.* Farmington Hills, MI: Greenhaven Press, 2009.

Hallam-Baker, Phillip. *dotCrime Manifesto: How to Stop Internet Crime.* Boston, MA: Pearson Education, 2008.

Harmon, Daniel E. *Careers in Internet Security.* New York, NY: Rosen Publishing, 2011.

Janvers, Eamon. *Broker, Trader, Lawyer, Spy: The Secret World of Corporate Espionage.* New York, NY: HarperCollins, 2010.

Miller, Michael. *Absolute Beginner's Guide to Computer Basics.* 5th ed. Indianapolis, IN: Que/Pearson Education, 2010.

Porterfield, Jason. *Careers as a Cyberterrorism Expert.* New York, NY: Rosen Publishing, 2011.

Romano, Amy. *Cool Careers Without College for People Who Love Everything Digital.* New York, NY: Rosen Publishing, 2007.

Soloman, Michael G., et al. *Computer Forensics JumpStart.* 2nd ed. Indianapolis, IN: Wiley, 2011.

Townsend, John. *Cyber Crime Secrets.* Mankato, MN: Amicus, 2012.

Brenner, Joel. *America the Vulnerable: Inside the New Threat Matrix of Digital Espionage, Crime, and Warfare.* New York, NY: Penguin Press, 2011.

Cimons, Marlene. "Cybersecurity: Training Students." *U.S. News & World Report,* May 29, 2012. Retrieved June 2012 (http://www.usnews.com/science/articles /2012/05/29/cybersecurity–training-students_print).

Douglas, John, and Johnny Dodd. *Inside the Mind of BTK: The True Story Behind the Thirty-Year Hunt for the Notorious Wichita Serial Killer.* Hoboken, NJ: Wiley, 2007.

Downing, Douglas, et al. *Dictionary of Computer and Internet Terms,* 10th Edition. Hauppauge, NY: Barron's, 2009.

Federal Bureau of Investigation. "Digital Forensics: Regional Labs Help Solve Local Crimes." FBI.gov, May 31, 2011. Retrieved July 2012 (http://www.fbi.gov/news/stories /2011/may/forensics_053111).

Federal Bureau of Investigation. "Most Wanted – Cyber Crimes." FBI.gov. Retrieved July 2012 (http://www.fbi .gov/wanted/cyber).

Garrett, G. M. (Senior Police Officer, Houston Police Department and FBI – Computer Crimes Task Force), interview with the author, July 19, 2012.

Higgins, Kelly Jackson. "Operation Shady RAT Attackers Employed Steganography." DarkReading.com, August 11, 2011. Retrieved June 2012 (http://www .darkreading.com/taxonomy/index/printarticle /id/231400084).

Kingsbury, Alex. "WikiLeaks Scandal Spurs Hackers vs. Lobbyist Fight." *U.S. News & World Report*, April 24, 2011. Retrieved August 2012 (http://www.usnews.com/news /articles/2011/04/24/wikileaks-scandal-spurs-hackers -vs-lobb).

Lichtblau, Eric. "Wireless Firms Are Flooded by Requests to Aid Surveillance." *New York Times*, July 8, 2012. Retrieved August 2012 (http://www.nytimes.com/2012/07/09 /us/cell-carriers-see-uptick-in-requests-to-aid-surveillance .html?pagewanted=all).

Lohr, Steve. "New Programs Aim to Lure Young into Digital Jobs." *New York Times*, December 21, 2009. Retrieved July 2012 (www.nytimes.com/2009/12/21/technology /21nerds.html?_r=1).

Maass, Peter, and Megha Rajogopalan. "That's No Phone. That's My Tracker." *New York Times*, July 15, 2012. Retrieved August 2012 (http://www.nytimes.com/2012 /07/15/sunday-review/thats-not-my-phone-its-my-tracker .html?_r=1).

McCoy, Lisa. *Computers and Programming*. New York, NY: Ferguson/Infobase Publishing, 2010.

Mitnick, Kevin. *Ghost in the Wires: My Adventures as the World's Most Wanted Hacker*. New York, NY: Little, Brown and Company, 2011.

National Institute of Justice. "Digital Forensics Training." NIJ.com. Retrieved May 2012 (http://www.nij.gov/nij /topics/forensics/evidence/digital/training/welcome.htm).

O'Deane, Matthew. "Combating Gangsters Online." FBI Enforcement Bulletin, April 2011, Vol. 30, Issue 4. Retrieved July 2012 (http://www.fbi.gov/stats-services

/publications/law-enforcement-bulletin/april_2011
/human_sex_trafficking).

Olson, Parmy. *We Are Anonymous: Inside the Hacker World of LulzSec, Anonymous, and the Global Cyber Insurgency.* New York, NY: Little, Brown and Company, 2012.

Orr, Bob. "Senate Bill Looks to Tighten Cyber Defenses." CBS News, August 1, 2012. Retrieved August 2012 (http://www.cbsnews.com/8301-18563_162-57484878 /senate-bill-looks-to-tighten-cyber-defenses/?tag=mncol;lst;1).

Robinson, James S. "Hunting the Craigslist Killer." *Phoenix,* April 4, 2012. Retrieved August, 6, 2012 (http//:thephoenix .com/boston/news/136636-hunting-the-craislist-killer).

Sanger, David. *Confront and Conceal: Obama's Secret Wars and Surprising Use of American Power.* New York, NY: Crown Publishing Group, 2012.

Shelly, Gary B., and Misty E. Vermaat. *Discovering Computers– Fundamentals.* Boston, MA: Course Technology/Cengage Learning, 2011.

Sher, Julian. *Caught in the Web: Inside the Police Hunt to Rescue Children from Online Predators.* New York, NY: Carroll & Graf, 2007.

Stein, Richard Joseph, ed. *Internet Safety.* New York, NY: H. W. Wilson, 2009.

Waggoner, Kim, ed. *FBI Handbook of Forensic Services.* Washington, DC: FBI Laboratory, 2007.

Index

A

Anonymous, 39

B

background checks, 44–45
BackTrack, 28
botnets, 36–37
Brenner, Paul, 33

C

Central Intelligence Agency (CIA),
    40, 45, 46, 59, 60, 61
cloud computing/storage, 14, 21
computer forensics
    educational/background
        requirements, 56–58, 61–63
    explanation of, 6–10
computer forensics techniques
    cell phones, 27–28
    e-mails, 26–27
    Internet searches, 26
    social networking media, 25–26
computer operation, basics of,
    10–14
computer security
    and corporate systems and
        networks, 51–53
    explanation of, 7, 32–34
cookies, 26
cyberterrorism, 7, 8, 51–52
cyber weapons/cyber warfare, 46–48

E

EnCase Forensic, 28
encryption, 6, 19, 40–42, 43
evidence
    analyzing, 22
    collecting and preserving, 17,
        18–21

F

Federal Bureau of Investigation
    (FBI), 19, 22, 30–31, 32, 36, 59,
    60, 61
federal jobs/internships, how to
    find, 59–60
"Flame" virus, 47
Forensic Toolkit, 28
fusion centers, 30

G

Garrett, Mike, 22–25, 30
global positioning systems (GPS), 5,
    8, 16, 27

H

hackers/hactivists, 8, 33–34, 37,
    38–39, 40, 51–52, 53, 54, 65–67
Hayden, Michael, 46
Henry, Shawn, 34
Higgins, Kelly Jackson, 43

L

law enforcement entities, cooperation among, 29–32

M

malware, 34–38, 43, 46, 51–52, 56
Markoff, Philip, 12
military service, as route to career in computer forensics, 63–65
Mitnick, Kevin, 39, 54, 55, 66

N

National Security Agency (NSA), 33, 40, 42, 45, 59

O

Olympic Games project, 46
Operation Shady RAT, 43

P

penetration testing, 53–55
Poulson, Kevin, 66–67
private investigators, 49–51

R

Rader, Dennis, 12
rootkit, 36

S

Sanger, David, 45, 46
spearphishing, 34
steganography, 40, 43
Stuxnet, 46–47

T

Trojan horse, 35

U

USB flash drives, 21

V

viruses, computer, 35

W

worms, computer, 35–36, 46

ABOUT THE AUTHOR

Writer and educator Terry Teague Meyer lives in Houston, Texas. A longtime fan of movies and television shows about law enforcement, she enjoyed learning how such entertainment distorts the truth about criminal investigation. After conducting research for this book, she has made computer security a much higher priority than before.

PHOTO CREDITS

Cover, p. 1 (background) © iStockphoto.com/Andrey Prokhorov; front cover (inset) Your lucky photo/Shutterstock .com; pp. 7, 15, 20, 35, 37, 47, 50, 52, 64 © AP Images; p. 9 New York Daily News Archives/New York Daily News/Getty Images; pp. 13, 41 AFP/Getty Images; p. 18 Bloomberg/ Getty Images; p. 23 Mike Garrett, Senior Police Officer, Houston Police Department; p. 31 Emmanuel Dunand/ AFP/Getty Images; p. 38 Sean Gallup/Getty Images; p. 41 Paul J. Richards/AFP/Getty Images; p. 55 SANS Institute; p. 57 Hill Street Studios/Blend Images/Getty Images; p. 66 Protegga LLC ™; interior page border image © iStockphoto .com/Daniel Brunner, pp. 12, 13, 23, 24, 36, 44, 45, 54, 59, 60 (text box background) © iStockphoto.com/Nicholas Belton.

Designer: Brian Garvey; Photo Researcher: Marty Levick